Praise for *What the Chickadee Knows*

"'Recognize yourselves in shared water,' writes Margaret Noodin in 'Apenimonodan' ('Trust') as the poems of *What the Chickadee Knows* open into an Anishinaabemowin world, asking us to listen, to be present in 'what we notice.' What I notice—what I delight in—is the music of poetry—visual and aural—how the sheer sound of words and each poem's visual lyricism creates meaning enough for connection. Poetry is music; poetry is the spirit of the senses sounded into life by breath. With these generous and rapt poems, written in Anishinaabemowin and translated by the author herself into English, Noodin gives us an extraordinary gift: an invitation into the illumination of language."

—Jennifer Elise Foerster

"With careful attention to rhythm and sound, *What the Chickadee Knows* reveals the wonderfully unexpected connections between Anishinaabemowin and English. Weaving together not only different languages but different landscapes and histories, this collection of evocative and minutely observed poems celebrates the vast web of relations that sustains us all."

—Adam Spry (White Earth Anishinaabe), assistant professor of writing, literature, and publishing, Emerson College

"Through nuanced connections, Margaret Noodin's poems partake in important Anishinaabeg world-making. Here observations of season and place always include human interaction: snowshoes 'writing canoe shapes in bright snow,' jam-makers 'mixing wind and shining water.' This collection—a primer on how to locate ourselves 'in the center of the blessed'—nevertheless assesses damage caused by America's exclusionary history, becomes 'a sneak-up dance of survival.'"

—Kimberly Blaeser, author of *Copper Yearning* and Wisconsin poet laureate 2015–16

"Would it be strange for me, strange of me, to tell you not to read but listen to these poems? There is so much silence and near silence within and between the words, the lines, the pages of this book. These poems, shaped of many languages, quieted me, and reminded me to listen—that listening requires my own quiet. So, as in any walk anywhere upon the earth, beneath the sky—or through this book—my quiet lead me to Noodin's deep silence, carried me to every important thing there was and is to hear."

—Mark Turcotte, author of *Exploding Chippewas*

What the Chickadee Knows

Great Lakes Books Series

A complete listing of the books in this series
can be found online at wsupress.wayne.edu

Editor

Thomas Klug
Sterling Heights, Michigan

What the Chickadee Knows

Gijigijigaaneshiinh Gikendaan

Poems

in Anishinaabemowin

and English

by Margaret Noodin

Wayne State University Press

Detroit

ISBN 978-0-8143-4750-8 (paperback)
ISBN 978-0-8143-4751-5 (e-book)

Library of Congress Control Number: 2020935123

Wayne State University Press
Leonard N. Simons Building
4809 Woodward Avenue
Detroit, Michigan 48201-1309

Visit us online at wsupress.wayne.edu

Gimiigwechiwi'inininim omaa ayaayeg gaa-wiidokawiyeg miinawaa ayaayeg gaagige-minawaanigoziwining.

Contents

Gaa-Ezhiwebag | History

Jibwaa Agindaman / Preface

Whether we hear *giji-giji-gaane-shii-shii* or *chick-a-dee-dee-dee* depends on how we have been taught to listen. Our world is shaped by the sounds around us and the filter we use to turn thoughts into words. Like the poems in *Weweni*, the lines and images here were conceived first in Anishinaabemowin and then in English. They are an attempt to hear and describe the world according to an Anishinaabe paradigm.

Anishinaabemowin is the language of the Odawa, Potawatomi, and Ojibwe people centered in the Great Lakes region. It is currently used in more than two hundred Anishinaabe communities in Quebec, Ontario, Manitoba, Saskatchewan, Alberta, North Dakota, Michigan, Wisconsin, and Minnesota. Like many indigenous languages, its vitality is precarious. Although some of our most beloved elders and teachers left us in recent years, the number of speakers is beginning to hold steady. I recall the early days of learning the language, when some argued it should not be written and no one spelled with consistency. Today I am challenged by a new generation of students working to use Ojibwemowin, Odawamowin, and Bodwewadmimwen in urban and rural places, at home, at work, and in cyberspace. They keep me focused and give me reason to push my own limits whenever possible. What we write today will be the bridge our future children have to the past.

The poems in my first book had the imprint of several dialectal landscapes that were part of my learning journey. In this book, I center my spelling and thoughts in the western Ojibwemowin I learned in the 1980s in Gakaabikaang near the confluence of the Minisota and Michizibi Rivers. The first section of the book illustrates the way Anishinaabemowin blends philosophy, science, and psychology while the second half traces less commonly known histories or provides a less common view of well-known events. I hope some readers find the gaps I left intentionally between the Anishinaabemowin and English translations to mark doorways between eras and worldviews.

A few practical facts bear repeating to encourage those not familiar with Anishinaabemowin to dive into a book filled with long lines in a new language. The spelling system used in this volume is called Fiero Double Vowel and was created by Charles Fiero and a group of Canadian speakers. Although this is the most common writing system in the southern Great Lakes region, there are syllabic alphabets, folk-phonetic systems, alternate spellings, and other vocabulary choices that make the language of each community distinct.

The poems are bursting with vowels and repeated syllables. To sound out the words, remember the following:

A single *a* sounds like the *u* in *cup*.
A double *aa* sounds like the *a* in *father*.
One *e* sounds like the *e* in the French word *café*.
One *i* sounds like the *i* in words like *bit*, *little*, *sip*.
Two *ii*'s sound like the *ee* or *ea* in *knee*, *peach*, or *each*.
A single *o* may sound like the *au* in *caught*, or the *u* in *put*.
A double *oo* sounds like the *oo*'s in *too*, *soon*, or *moon*.

Consonants represent the same sounds as in English, but *f*, *l*, *r*, *v*, and *x* are never used. There are also consonant clusters: sk, shp, sht, shk, mb, and nd.

At any time of year near Michigaming, the Freshwater Sea, we might hear *giji-giji-gaane-shii-shii* with more *shii-shii* to add intensity when needed. There is much to fear in our century as humans are learning hard lessons about balance and greed, but there is also great joy to be found in the bitter taste of pine needles, memories of ones who knew the stars, and open hearts of the ones we trust. It is my hope that these poems, like the *gijigijigaaneshi-ishii*, also called by some a chickadee, will stay with you in all seasons.

E-Maaminonendamang
What We Notice

Bangan Zoogipoog

Epiichi bangan zoogipoog
biinijichaagigewaad
biidaazhegaamewaad
endazhi maaminonendamang
ezhi-oshkibaakadawaabiyang waaseyaabang.

Silent Snowfall

While silently the snow falls
souls are washed new
arriving along the shore
where we pause to consider
the way each dawnlight opens our eyes again.

Gijigijigaaneshiinh

Ningii-ozhibii'amawaag gijigijigaaneshiinyag onzaam gaawiin maajaasiiwaad miinawaa Linda LeGarde Grover gii-ozhibii'aad Azhegiiwe Wiingashk.

Aanikoobijiganag aanikoobidoowaad wiingashk wiindamawiyangidwa gashkibijigeg gegashk-akiing.

Gijigijigaaneshiinh ayaa gawaandag noondaagozid noondenimiyangidwa manidookeyaang manidoowiyaang.

Chickadee

For the chickadees who never leave, and for Linda LeGarde Grover, who wrote about them in The Road Back to Sweetgrass.

The ancestors tied and extended it
the sweetgrass, telling us
make bundles, the world is not yet ripe.

The marsh chickadee is there in the white pine
calling out, wanting to be with us
it's a ceremony, a way to be alive.

Bi Booniig

Boonipon apii biboong miidash dakaanimad odishiwe
    daashkikwaading
Boonitamaang madwezigoshkaag miinawaa bizindaamangidwaa
    wewenjiganoozhiinhyag
Boonigidetaadiwag mii maajii-aamiwaad epiichi
    makwamiiwaagamaag
Booniiwag enaazhi-zhingobiiwaadikwanan nanegaaj
    waaboozwaagonagaag
Boonam gegapii miidash boonendang aki biinish bookoshkaag

Landing Here

When it stops snowing in winter and deep cold arrives to crack the
      ice
We stop hearing the freezing then listen for the great horned owls
They forgive one another and begin to mate while the world is
      frozen
Landing on pine branches as snow falls gently in large flakes
Eventually she lays an egg then ignores the world until it breaks

Agoozimakakiig Idiwag

Ishkwaa biboon bii'omigag
gaawiin geyabi aabita-
nibwaakaamashkawajisiiwaad
biibaagiyaang ani biibaagiyang.

Naami-zaasijiwanagek
agoozimakakiig gii ningiziyang
mii noopimidoodeyang mashkiigong
biibaagiyaan ani biibaagiyan.

Dibishkoo didibaashkaa
zhaabwibiisaag zoogipoog
ziigwang ziibiskaaj miidash
biibaagiyan ani biibaagiyaan.

Epichii maadaa'ogoyang basweweyang
beshoganawaabmigag aawiyang
waasaganawaabmigag aawiyang
biibaagiyang ani biibaaginidiyaang.

What the Peepers Say

After the winter waiting
no longer half-
frozen by design
our calling becomes all calling.

Under the rippling bark
peepers have thawed
to crawl into the swamp where
my calling becomes your calling.

A seismic seiche
a synaptic snowstorm
of springtime repetition and
your calling becomes my calling.

As we drift away on our echoes
we are the details
we are the distance and
all calling becomes our calling.

Umpaowastewin

Ningii-mikwenimaag Chibinesi-ban ezhi-aabajitood ikidowinan
miinawaa Umpaowastewin ezhi-baashkiminsiganiked epiichi o'o
ozhibii'amaan. Umpaowastewin idamang Miikawaadizi-Biidaabanokwe
Bwaanimong mii dash izhinikaazod Pat Northrup.

Ode'iminibaashkiminasiganke
ginagawinad wiishko'aanimad, waaseyaagami
miinawaa gipagaa nibwaakaa,
bigishkada'ad, dibaabiiginad
gakina gaa-zhawenimangidwa
gakina gaa-wani'angidwa
nagamowinan waa-nagamoyaang
miigwanag waa-wawezhi'angidwa
ezhi-zhoomiingweyaangoba
mooshkine moodayaabikoong
ji-baakaakonid apii bakadeyaang
boozangwaamaang biboong besho
gaa-oginiig endazhi-ginibigiwaad.

Daybreak Woman

I was remembering Jim Northrup, the word-crafter, and Pat Northrup, the jam-maker, while writing this. Umpaowastewin *means* "beautiful daybreak woman" *in the Dakota language and is the name given to Pat Northrup.*

She makes strawberry jam
mixing sweet wind and shining water
with thick wisdom
pounding, measuring
everything we've cared for
everything we've lost
the songs we have not yet sung
the feathers yet to decorate
and all the ways we've smiled
into jars filled to the brim
to be opened when we are thin
sleeping deeply in winter near
where the tomatoes once grew.

Gimaazinibii'amoon

Ningikendaan akiin bakaanag
onzaam gaa nindaanikoobijiganinaanig mazinibii'amawaawaad
onzaam wiijiwag wanishinowaad daawaad noongom
onzaam gii-izhi'iyan zhigo.

Giishkaanaabikaa ina gidaaw
gaye gichigami aawiyaan
gemaa washkiyaanimaazoyaan
gaawiin gikenimisiiyan?

A Message to You

I know there are different worlds
because our ancestors sent them messages
because lost lovers now live in them
because you just said that right now.
Are you the carved shoreline
and I the sweet water sea
or am I the shifting wind
you cannot perceive?

Ishkodensan

Indagindaas, agindaasoyaan
gii-zegimiyan
gaashaabikidowinan
aandeg dazhwaanged.

Diba'iganens, diba'igan
gaawiin ningii-enendansiin
ji-maaminonendamaan
ishkodensan gii-dakonaman.

Giginjiba'in ginjidamaan
negwaakwaajigan indodeng
giba'amaan bagonewin
jibwaa-onjigaa'aanimiziyaan.

Baashkide, baashkine
mii bagosendamaan
wii ezhi-meshkwaadooyaan
bwaa-minjinaweziyaan.

Matches

I am counting, counting
the way you scare me
with sharp iron words
a crow spreading wings.
A minute, a mile
I didn't think
to notice
the matches you were holding.
I flee you, pounding
the tap back into my heart
plugging the hole
before my fear leaks.
Explosion, expiration
and now I hope
for a way to trade
without regrets.

Zoongizaagi'idiwin

Aabitaa-dibiki-wewe animaanimizi
aazhobizod aanakwaagamig
wewemo-enendang
. . . baashkiziganan
. . . wishkobii-manoomin
. . . gaye giimoodag
mii dash biida'amaazod bizaanabing
ezhi-zoongide'ed ishkwaa zegizid mii dash
googiid ziibing ji-zhaaboshkaachiged.

Fierce Love

The midnight goose goes away in fear
flying across a sea of clouds
thinking in a goose language of
. . . guns
. . . sweet wild rice
. . . and secrets
then arrives singing into the silence
of the strength that comes after being afraid
diving into the river to sift again.

Apenimonodan

Apenimonodan gikendaman
aanind bemaadizijig
waa-goshko'iwaad
bamendamowaad akiing
bamenimaawaad asabikeshiinan
bamenimiwaad ge-giin
bakiseyan mii gibaakwa'igeyan
miidash bakiseyan miinawaa.
Waasikwa'agwaa ezhi-waaseziwaad.
Nisidawinaadiyeg ojichaagobiishin.

Trust

Trust that you know
some people
who will surprise you
with the way they care for the world
and every small spider
the way they care for you
as you open and shut
then open again.
Polish the way they shine.
Recognize yourselves in shared water.

Miikindizi Baapaawinad

Chibenesi dibaajimo, baapaajimo
ezhi-niimiwaad aandegoog gaashkaading ziigwang
ezhi-ikidowinan-nooshkaachinaganiked niibinong
ezhi-mikawaad mekwendaagozijin dagwaaging
miidash gikinoo'amawiyangid Anishinaabe-aadizookeyaang
biboong.

Teasing Shakery

Great Bird narrates, comediates
the way crows dance on a crust of snow in spring
the way he makes baskets for word winnowing in summer
the way he finds memory veterans in fall
then teaches us to tell tales the Anishinaabe way in winter.

Jichibakozh Jichaag

Gibagidinaan zanagak,
jichaagowazisoniken.
Gijichibakozhaa jichaag
asiginaman anoonji gegoon.
Gaawiin waabandansiinaawaa
akiing gaye mitigong
aazhidetamowinan wewebaasinoog.

Ezhi-mino-anwebiyang
Ezhi-minjimininjiizhidiyang.

Gibagidinaan zegaanakwag
mii dash zhawenimegwaa.
Baakaakonan ishkwaandeman
mewinzha gii-gibaakwa'aman.
Gakina waa-waabandaanaawaa
ishkwaakidesagoon
waakaabimaadiziwining

Rock Your Soul

Release impossibilities
build a nest for your soul.
Rock your soul inside
the space you have gathered.
What they don't see
on the ground and in the trees
are the answers swaying.

As we find peaceful sleep.
As we connect our dreams.

Release the dark storms
and you will be blessed.
Fill the emptiness behind
all the doors you once closed.
Then they will see
the bright embers
that protect our lives.

Waanimazinbii'iganike

Ningii-ozhibii'amawaa Daphne Odjigiban.

Gimaajaamin ina gemaa maajitaayang igo
apii dibaajimoyang anaami-madogaaning?
Gidizhinaagwi'aanaanig ina gimishomisinaanig miinawaa
    gookomisinaanig?
Giwaabamaanaanig ina naasaab aanzheniig gaye Gichidebenjiged?
Ginisidawaabandaamin ina wiigwaasenaandeg,
oziigiwaabigwaniin gaye amooshimowin?
Gibizindawaanaan ina baapaase baapaagaakwa'aad
    akikaandagibanan?
Gigikendaamin ina maamawigaabawiyang mooka'ang?
Ginisidawendaamin megwaaj aanjiseyang
bingwiwiyang, biisibiisaawiyang.
Anaami-madogaaning apii dibaajimoyang
maajitaayang miinawaa maajaayang igo.

Writing Images in Circles

Written for Daphne Odjig.

Are we taking leave or taking off
when we tell stories under the stars?
Do we look like our grandfathers and grandmothers?
Do we see the same angels and Creator?
Do we recognize the color of birch,
the wrinkle of leaves and dance of bees?
Do we hear the woodpecker pecking on the dead pine?
Do we know to stand together at sunrise?
Do we understand that as we change
we are the sand, we are the showers?
As we tell stories beneath the stars
we are beginning and we are moving on.

Gimanaajitoomin Nibi

Gimanaajitoomin nibi
aabijijiwang akiing miziweshkaag
bi-basweweg, ni-basweweg
mookijiwang baabimoseyang.

Gimanaaji'aanaan Nookomis Nibi-giizis.
Gimanaaji'aanaanig giizisoog
nookizid ookomis waasaabikizod,
mindidod mishoomis jaagaakizod.

Baanimaa biidaanamoyang biidaabang
mii maajinanaandawi'iwe-nagamoyang
bagaka'amaazoyang, aabida'amaazoyang
naadamaageyang nagamong.

Gizhaabowemin ezhi-zhaabwiiyang
odaminowinan ozhitooyang, mazinitooyang
aanikenootawangwaa dewe'iganag gaye zhiishiigwanag
mino-mgondaaganewaad mino-anishinaabeyang.

We Honor Water

We honor the liquid
the entire flowing watershed
echoing here and there
water infusing our path.

We honor her silver brilliance.
We honor both night and day suns
soft grandmother reflecting,
great grandfather burning.

After a breath dawns within us
and a healing song begins
we sing clearly and constantly
in the service of sound.

We accompany our survival
with games creating, arranging,
translating for drums and rattles
to animate the sound of being good beings.

Bemaadizijig gaa-gizhenindaagoziwag ji-zaagi'igowaad.

Gegoon gaa-gizhenindaagwadoon ji-aabajichigaadeg.

Noongom gegoon onzaam zaagitoowaad gaye bemaadizijig
aabaji'igowaad . . .

. . . wenji majizhewebag.

Tenzin Gyatso, Midaaswi-ashi-niiwaching Dalai Lama

Bemaadizijig

Ji-zaagi'angidwaa, ji-zaagi'iyangidwaa.

Agaami-zaaga'igan zaagidawejiwang
Gizhemanido gizheninjige
gakina gegoon be-bezhig
giizhig, giizis, giizhaabikizid,
gizhendamowinan gaye gizhinaakonigewinan
mii dash epiichi giiwitaashkaamagag
gizhenindizoyaang
ji-zaagi'angidwaa, ji-zaagi'iyangidwaa
ji-mikamaang, ji-mikwendamaang
gakina gegoon ezhi-aabajichigaadeg
ji-mikawangidwaa, ji-mikwenimangidwaa
be-bezhig bemaadizijig ezhi-zhaawenimangidwaa
minisan giishkijigwenaag gichigaming
maang-anongan zagaakwa'igaazonid giizhigong.

People were created to be loved.

Things were created to be used.

Today things are loved and people are used . . .

. . . this is the reason for bad happenings.

Tenzin Gyatso, the 14ᵗʰ Dalai Lama

The Ones Alive

To love and be loved.
Across the lake openings begin
the Creator creates
all things one by one,
the sky, the sun, the moon being full
decisions and rules
then amidst the turning cycles
we create ourselves
to love and be loved
to find and to remember
the use for everything
to find and remember
the singular blessing of every being
the way every island is embraced by the sea
the way the north star is held by the sky.

Nindaanikanootaanan Gikaadendamowinan

Nindaazhidemaa Meg Day ishkwaa gii-ozhibii'ang *Giikaadadendagwad Aanikanootagwak.*

Boonigidetawishin
boonigidetawishinaam
gaawiin noondansiimaang
    noondaagoosiiyan
ezhi-niibawiyan zoogipong sa
giizis igo ge-niisibizhad mii dash
ge-nagwaadaman ji-mikwendaman
naawayi'iing zesegaandagwadabiin gaye wadikwanan
odoonan, oshkiinzhigoon, otawagan gaye niisiigininjaanan,
ingiw ozhaawashkowewegwaned
aagawaateshkaag ombiigweweg
ge-noojimotooyan biboong gaye
odibaajimowiniwaan mindimooyenyag
ge-noojimotooyan ezhi-nisidotaadiyang
wewebaazhimoyang
mikomiyan, mikomiyang
mashkawaakwading
mii miinawaa "debwetaagoziyang"
nasab nitaagwag "dibendaagoziyang"
ombaabateg,
ombaaniteg ombaashiyang.

Translation of an Elegy

A response to "Elegy in Translation" by Meg Day.

Forgive me,
forgive us all,
for not hearing that
    not hearing you
the way you stand in the snow
as you draw down the sun
setting snares for memories
between spruce roots and branches
lips, eyes, ears, and fingers
blue feathers, green feathers waving
casting shadows loud and clear
your cure for winter and
old wives' tales
your cure for wounds of meaning
a language of motion
reminding me, reminding us
water is solid sometimes
and "we are telling the truth"
sounds like "we belong"
the way smoke rises up
a mirage we can ride.

Jiikimaadizi

Apii Manidoo-giizisoons basangwaabid
gaye gaawiin bazhiba'ansiimaan
ge-bimaadagendamaan dwaa'ibaaning
mii mikwendamaan Ode'imini-giizis
miskwiiwid miskwaawaasiged giizhigong.

Dagwaagin apii waaboozoog zaagi'agwaa
idash gaawiin dakonaasiiwagwaa
napaajinaanzowayeyaang
waawaashkeshikwe mikwenimag
ziikipidang ziibiwan ji-gidagaakoonsiked.

Wenpanad gwayakowendamang,
zhaabwaabiyang, bakobiiseyang
zanagak gwenibiiyang,
akawaabiyang, bakegaabawiyang
ji-mikamang ezhi-jiikimaadiziyang.

A Joyful Life

When the sky's eye blinks in December
and I can't spear one of the
thoughts swimming past the ice hole
I think of the strawberry-moon light
bleeding across a long summer day.

When I fall in love with autumn rabbits
but can't hold them close enough
and all our fur is the wrong color
I think of deer woman
drinking rivers to make spotted fawns.

It's easy to change our minds
to look through a window, fall into a lake
it's harder to quit,
to wait or step off the main path
to discover a joyful life.

Naabibii'aan Agoodeg

Omaada'adoon ziigwan-mazina'igan
anaamayi'ii baashkabigiizhigong
gaye apane dibiki-giizisan basangwaabinid
mii abid ningide-niibinong.

Onaabibii'aan ziiginigaadenig ziibiin
zhaabwayi'ii endazhi-baashkaabigwaniinig
niibina-enaandenig maamawaginjigewinan
waawaagitigweyaakwaang.

Imaa epiichi-maamwibemaadizijig
aaboozikadendizowaad
agawaatesewaad gaye waaseyaaziwaad
mikamaang agoodeg.

Tracing Balance

She follows the map of spring
under the sky's one bursting eye
and the ever-blinking moon
into the melt of summer.

He traces the pouring river
through blossoms bursting
multicolored equations
winding into the woods.

There while society
turns itself inside out
the shadow and the shining
find balance.

Gaawiin o'o Dibendaagwasinoon

Gigaganoonidimin dash gaawiin noozhesiiyang
Gidozhitoomin dash gaawiin naabesiiyang
Gaawiin o'o dibendaagwasinoon

Ge-ningide wadiswan
Gidagindaamin mitigoonsan
Gigiziibiiginaamin azhashki

Nindakonaanaanig asiniig
Gidombiwebinaanaanig ezhi-enaanzowaad
Gaawiin noondeyaabaagwasinoon ziibiwan

Ge-bawaakide giizhig dibikong
Gimbasangaabibani`omin
Gidasoozomin waasamowining

None of This Belongs Here

We talk and no one is female
We build and no one is male
None of this belongs here

As the nest melts
We are counting sticks
We are washing mud

We hold onto stones
We toss their color into the air
None of the rivers are thirsty

The day burns a hole in the night
We close both eyes suddenly
We are trapped in the lightning

Izhise

Ogii-inendaan wanising giizhig dibikong
azhigwa waabandang aazhogan aawang
bi-aazhogeyang, ni-aazhogeyang
mii agwaashimiyangidwa biidaabang
megwaa waagoshag aazhikwewaad.

Mii goshkozi nandawaabamaad
gaa-gikenimaad jibwaa
aanjised, aanjisenid
debibidood gaagiigido-biiwaabikoons
inaakonang waa-ezhiwebag noongom.

Waa-wenda-ishkwaase
ge-gezika-nisidotamang
bangibiisaag, animibiisaag
gaye aabitaa-dibikag
dibishkoo naawakwe-giizhigag.

Time Flight

She used to think of night as a lost day
now she sees it is a bridge
for us to cross and recross
as we are saving each dawn
by the foxes screaming.

And he wakes up looking for
the one he knew before
one of them changed
grabbing a telephone
to chart the course of the new day.

All of this will end
with sudden insight
the way rain passes
and midnight is
like noon.

Waawaashikeshii-diba'iganeg

Gimikwenimin giiweyamban
mii bagami-ayaayan dibikong
miijiyan gaa-asanjigooyan
zhiiwitaagan gidenaniwing
wiishkobinendaman
debisiniiyan gaye onji-noondeshinan
gii-wiijikiwenimad gaye ojaanimitaayan.

Nimaaminonendaan waa-ezhiwebag
giishpin biminizhag oniijaaniw i'iwedi
gaawiin tesiinog aasamisag
daa-meshkwadooyaang miishaabiwinaanan
gemaa daa-baapizhimangidwaa pa'iinsan
mii mikwenimangidwaa ayaabeyan
gaye bimosaadamaang ji-mamaanjinoyaang.

At the Hour of the Deer

I think of you crossing toward home
becoming a part of the night
eating what was stored before
salt on the tongue
sweet satisfaction
satisfied and exhausted
by friendship and a full life.

I wonder briefly what would happen
if I followed the doe and
to where there is no visible wall
we could exchange lashes
we could laugh with the wood ones
remembering the bucks
and practicing a bit of magic.

Gaa-Ezhiwebag
History

Babeji-aanjisemigad

Gaabiboonoke gii-jiisibidoon gichigami
neyaashiiwang, neyaakobiiwang, neyaakwaag
biindig zaaga'iganing, agwajiing akiing.

Omaa zhawenimiyangidwa epiichi
agwaayaashkaag mii dash animaashkaag
gaye basweweg zisibimaadiziyaang.

Maamapii gidanishinaabemotaagoonaan
ginwenzh biboonagag, niibinong nitaawiging,
babeji-aanjisemigag apane.

A Gradual Flowing Transformation

The great sea was pinched by the glaciers
land reaching, water pointing, trees leaning
inside the lake, outside the land.

It is here we are loved
by the slow swell of tides
that echo the rasp of our lives.

This place speaks to us
of long winters, summer growth,
and slow constant change.

Niizhosagoons gemaa Nisosagoons
Daso-biboonagadoon

Ishkwaa gaa-ningaabikide
mikwaamiikaag ajina mii dash
daashkikwading, bagonezigwaag
ziibiins ani ziibi ziibiskaaj
ziigibiig ziigwanindagwag
wiindigoon zaaginizhikawaad gaye
ge-jiichiibiingwed mooz-anang
nagadenindinid bemaadizijin miziwe ziibiing.

Two or Three Thousand Years

After the minerals melted
ice reigned for a while and then
cracks and holes appeared
streams became a river casually
pouring seasons onto the land
wiindigoos were chased away by
the blink of a sky-moose's eye
lives were entwined along the Mississippi.

Izhi-aazhogeng

Ningii-ozhibii'aan ishkwaa babaamoseyaang Aztalan Gitigaan niin
miinawaa Chad Allen.

Nimbabimosemin maazinibikwakamigong
wegodogwen giishphin waabamiyangidwaa
ezhi-bimikaweyaang
ezhi-ezhininjiishinaang
biiwiwebinamaang ikidowinan, inenimowinan
aabitaa-giizizamaang aanikanootamaagewinan
gaye wanitamaang
zayaagi'iwejig gaa-ningizowaagwen gemaa
gebaakwa'igaazojig baaniiwiwaagwen.
Gaawiin igo ningikendanziimin mii minik
gaa-giizhenindamowaad
izhi-aazhogeng
gaa-giizhenimaawaad
zhingaabewasiniin
asinikaag ani-bingwikaag ani-nibikaag
bangitoowaad memeshkwad miigaadiwaad
waanadinaag ezhi-nisidotaadiyaang
mizhishawaang anaami-giizhigong.

Paths into the Past

Written after a walk with Chad Allen at Aztalan State Park.

We walk along the earth drawings
wondering if we are seen
leaving footprints
leaving handprints
scattering words and ideas
half-baked translations
and misunderstandings
where lovers might have melted or
prisoners became slaves.
We don't know how many
created this
path into the past
created these
messages in stone
soil turning to sand turning to water
vacillation between quiet and uprising
lacunas of understanding
left wide open to the sky.

Wanaanimizimigad

Gaawiin jiichiigwanjigesiiwag
jaachiibiingwenijig.
Gaawiin gondansiinaawaa
beshkodowezhijig.
Gaawiin maaminonendansiinaawaa
ojiibikan aawiyaang.
Gaawiin nisidotansiinaawaa
gikinoowizhangid ziibii.
Waagoshag waagaashiwag
gojimaandamowaad jiigaakwaang.
Waabizheshi geyabi bezhig onjida
o'amawaan waawaabiganoojiiyan.
Zhagashkaandaweg nanaakonaawaad
wenibaashkijigaazojig.
Biniskwaabiiginamigad
gaa-maajitamigag.

A Time of Confusion

They don't gnaw
the ones who wink.
They don't swallow
the ones who skin.
They don't notice
we are roots.
They don't understand
we guide the river.
Bent in the wind, the foxes
sniff the edge of the tree line.
The pine marten eats
one more mouse on purpose.
The squirrels have declared war
on the lost ones who explode.
The unraveling
has begun.

Mamaangaashkaa Michigaming

Nimikwenimaanaan Angelique Le Roy gii-ondaadizid 1766 miinawaa
gii-aawid oozhishen Menominee-ogimaa Ahkenepawehyan, wiiwan Jacques
Vieux-an gaye ogashiwid Minowakiing, Wisconsin.

Mamaangaashkaa besho Michigaming
gii-animaa'ang ezhi-bimaadiziyaang mewenzha
animaa'ogoyaang zhaawanong
maadaa'ogoyaang zhooniiyaashkaag.

Gii-madweyaashkaa apii maajiiwiidigeyaang
gii-ditibaashkaag apii abinoojikeyaang
niibina biboonan gii-giniginamowaad
Ojibweg, Mamaceqtawak, Bodwewadmik.

Mii gii-biidaashkaa mii adaaweyaang
mii aanjisemigag apane akiing
miinawaa awashime zinagag ji-bawaajigeyaang
waasa agwaayaashkaag ningaabii'anong.

The Surging Sea

In memory of Angelique Le Roy, born in 1766, granddaughter of Menominee leader Ahkenepaweh, wife of Jacques Le Vieux, and mother of Minowakiing, Wisconsin.

On the surging shores of Lake Michigan
it drifted away, the way we used to live
we also drifted, south
on waves of silver.

We heard the swell as our life began together
the rolling tides of making children
for many years mixing
Ojibwe, Menominee, Potawatomi.

Then on waves of trade
the earth forever changed
and dreaming is more difficult
on the other side of the western break.

Bingwi-nanaandawi'iwe-nagamowin

Mii o'o aanikoobijigaade gaa-ezhiwebag 1850 Gaa-mitaawangaagamaag
Oodena mitigwaakwaang daawaad Anishinaabeg besho Gichigaming
miinawaa gaa-ezhiwebag 1864 Heséovó'eo'hé'ke (Mitaawangaa-ziibiins)
daawaad Tsėhéstáno besho Ho'honáevo'omēnėstse (Asiniiwajiwan).

Anaambiig, anaamaabik
mikwendamang giizhigoon mikwenimangwaa
gaa-mewinzha aayaazha'osewaad
gichimookomaanakiing
zhimaaganishiwigamigoons
mii baabii'owaad, mii zhigajibii'owaad
bakadewaad miidash gawanaandamowaad
bedosewaad, majiwaapinewosewaad
gwejigiiwewaad.

Anaambiig, anaamaabik
mikwendamang giizhigoon mikwenimangwaa
gaa mewinzha gabeshiwaad akawaabiwaad besho
gichimookomaanakiing
besho zhimaaganishigamig
mii babaamademowaad, mii animademowaad
animinizhimowaad miinawaa giishkishinowaad
nitamawindwaa, majiwaapinewosewaad
gaawiin wiikaa giiwesiiwaad.

Anaambiig, anaamaabik
mikwendamang giizhigoon mikwenimangwaa,
gaa-mewinzha bagadinamowaad
Gaa-mitaawangaagamaang, Heséovó'eo'hé'ke
Gichigamig, Ho'honáevo'omēnėstse
noondawangwaa, nagamotawangwaa
ezhi-inawewaad inawemangwaa

A Sandy Healing Song

*This poem connects what happened in 1850 in Sandy Lake, in the woodlands
where the Anishinaabeg live near the Great Lakes, and what happened in
1864 in Sand Creek, where the Cheyenne live near the Rocky Mountains.*

Under the water, under the rock
we remember the days, we remember the ones
who long ago walked to and from
the long-knifed American
place of war, of distribution
then waited, became impatient
hungry then starving
walking, slowly dying
trying to go home.

Under the water, under the rock
we remember the days, we remember the ones
who long ago made camp in expectation near
the long-knifed American
place of war, of distribution
then crying away from there
ran terrified and falling in slices
murdered, slowly dying
never to go home.

Under the water, under the rock
we remember the days, we remember the ones
who long ago made offerings to
Sandy Lake, Sand Creek
the Great Sea, the Rocky Mountains
we hear them, we sing to them
they were our relations

ganawenindizowaad endazhi-bakaaniziwaad
giiwe-gizhibaabizowaad apane.

Anaambiig, anaamaabik
mikwendamang giizhigoon mikwenimangwaa
megwaa gabeshiwaad akawaabiwaad
oshki-gichi-akiing ayaawaad
gimoozikaw-zhaabwii-niimi'idiwaad
onaakonigewaad ezhi-nagamowinikewaad
nanaandawi'iwe-nagamowin
gaawiin wiikaa wanendansiimowaad
apane bi-giiwewaad.

caring across one another's differences
spinning always home.

Under the water, under the rock
we remember the days, we remember the ones
who right now make camp in expectation
in a new global space
a sneak-up dance of survival
they decide how to create
a healing song
never forgetting
always coming home.

Mooningwanekaaning

Mooningwane moona'ige
zhaaboshkaatood wiiyagasenong
moonaad manidoonsan
moonenimigod enigoonsan
okoonzh jiichiigibidood
niibinong noogishkaad
maaminonendang ezhi-ozhitood
mooningwanewazison
giimoodad getemitigong
minising gichigaming
gii-bimibatoonid Madaninibanan
gii-onjibaanid Gichi-weshkiibanan
Mooningwanekaaning.

Madeline Island

The flicker is digging
sifting the dust
inspecting the insects
suspected by ants
beak-scratching a mark
in the summer stopping place
considering construction
of a flicker's nest
secretly in an old tree
on an island in the sea
where Madeline strolled
home of the Great Renewer
home of the Flicker.

Mazinaazod Oshki-miin-gamigong

Awiya weweni ogii-onagoodoonan dibikaabaminaagwadong
biidaasmabiwaad gichi-wiindamaagewin
gaa-dibaajimotaagoowaad gakina bimaadizijin
"gaawiin zhawenjigesiiwaad bagwanawaadisiwaad"
. . . aanawi giizis eta gaawiin gwayakosidoon.

Gimikwenimigo Saymin gidozaawibabagiwayaanim biizikaman
ogozisimiwaa Getezi gaye Zaagigwiniing aawiyan
oozhisimaasim Ogimaa Dokimabi aawiyan
aanikoobjiganim Ogimaa Naniingibonzow aawiyan
. . . aanawi ogimaa gaawiin aawisiiyan gii-daawaad.

Besho giishpin biminizha'igeyang bebikaan miikanang
aasama-mazina'igansing mikwendaagozinid
gaa-ozhibii'aanid jaaginazhaawaad
niiwo-giizhigoon jibwaa Maakogidig
. . . aanawi izhibii'amawaanid niijaanisan.

Omaa tenoon gete-mazina'iganan gaye mazinaazowinan
naanagadawendamang ezhi-nisodotamang
mikaajigaadeg miinawaa mikaajigaazoyang
bagaksidooyang miinawaa wayezhingeyang
. . . aanawi gonemaa indaawaaj waa-mikaadiyang.

Portrayed in the Newberry

Someone has carefully hung them in the half-light
facing a declaration
that tells all the world the facts of
"the merciless Indian savages"
. . . but only the month is wrong.

We remember you, Simon, wearing your brown shirt
you are son of Elizabeth and Leopold
you are grandson of Chief Topinabee
you are great-grandson of Chief Naniquiba
. . . but you are not a "chief," they say.

Nearby if we follow a different road
a wall-card remembers one
who called for human extermination
four days before Wounded Knee
. . . but he wrote stories for children.

Here where there are old pages and portraits
we wonder how to understand
discovery and being discovered
clarification and collusion
. . . but maybe it is time instead to discover one another.

Oshki-Niibaa-anama'aa Gete-akiing

Aambe miskobineshiinh
ogiji-ayaayang bimaagonagaag biboong
anami'aadaa epiichi boonaanimag.

Gaaskanazodaa
ishpaa-ayaayang gaawaandagoog
ishpaandaweyang giizhigong.

Bagosendandaa gakina
awiiya gashki-noondaadiwaad
bakaani'anama'aa-nagamowaad.

Maajaadaa omaa ingoding
maada'azhang naasaab anang
jiibay-miikanang waabamang.

New Christmas in the Old World

Come along, cardinal,
over winter's wing
let's pray while the world is still.

Let's whisper
above the evergreens
climb high in the heavens.

Let's hope all
souls are able to hear
different hymns.

Let's leave here eventually
following the same star
we all see in the milky way.

Winiiam Aagimike

Ge-maajimamaangadepon
giizis ishpaagoozid, ishpaagonagaag agwajiing
mii dash inaaginang ezhi-inendang
naagadawendang debwemigag
gaye gaawiin debwesiinog
Skadi'an gaye Bakewizian naagadawenimaad
ezhi-gii-babaamaagimenid.

Chiwenipanad gii-wenji-aagimiked
miigwechiwi'aad aagimaakoon
waazhaabiid miidash waaginaang,
aazheyaajimowinan gashka'oodeg
gaa-nisidotamang inakamigag
gete-aadizookaanag gashka'oozowaad
ezhi-Gizhemanidoo naago'idizod.

Apii gii-giizhiitaad anokiid gaye bengoziwaad
giizikang makazinan mii biizikawaad aagiman
mii bineshiinhikaazod ji-babaamikawed
jiimaanibii'ang bagakaagonagaag
epiichi baazhida'ang ziibiwan
jiimaanibii'aad maazikamikwe
gaye ode'eng zhawenimaad.

William Making Snowshoes

As frozen flakes fell in clusters
sun high in the sky, snow deep outside
he began to bend his thoughts
considering what is true
and what is not
considering Skadi and Pukwiss
and the way they walked on the snow.

Because it was simplest, he made snowshoes
thanked the black ash
cut the laces and bent the wood,
all of the old stories tangling
what we understand happened
all of the old stories tangling
the way the Creator is revealed.

When his work was done and they were dry
he took off his moccasins, put on the snowshoes
going out to leave tracks light as a bird
writing canoe shapes in the bright snow
as he walked over rivers
writing kiss shapes on the earth
and in the center of the blessed.

Aaniin Idamang?

Inyan Woslata, 2016. Mní wichóni.

Aaniin idamang gaa-ezhiwebag
mashkodeng gii-mashkawiziwaad
bebezhig okoshimaawaad asiniiwan
endazhi-mashkosiikaag?

Minogizhebaawagad. Anpétu kin dé wasté.

Aaniin idamang ge-ezhiwebag
ji-zhooniyaakewaad onji-ziinibiizhaawaad
bibagasiniiwan biinish miskwiiwid aki
aanjitoowaad makade-bimide?

Minogizhebaawagad. Anpétu kin dé wasté.

Aaniin idamang ge-ezhiwebag
ganawenimaawaad mashkode-bizhiikiwag
mashkode-akakojiishan niiminid
Ojig-Anang madogaaning Ogimaa?

Minogizhebaawagad. Anpétu kin dé wasté.

Aaniin idamang waa-ezhiwebag
giishpin gaawiin nisidotawaasiigwaa
Chimookimanag Ochéti Sakówin-an?
Gaawiin aate'siinoon o'o biidaaban.

Minogizhebaawagad. Anpétu kin dé wasté.

How Do We Speak of This?

Standing Rock, 2016. Water is life.

How do we speak of what has happened
in the prairie where they were strong
one by one piling stones
in the long grass?

It is a good day.

How do we speak of what is happening
as they make money squeezing
layers of stone until
the earth bleeds oil?

It is a good day.

How do we speak of what is happening
as buffalos watch over
prairie dogs dancing
on the Chief's constellation?

It is a good day.

How do we speak of what will happen
if there is no understanding between
the Long Knives and the Seven Fires?
This dawn cannot be extinguished.

It is a good day.

Ishkwaa Biinjwebinige

Omaa Gichimookomaanakiing
anishinaabewiyang gaye naabishkaageyang
wiikwaji'oyang gaye odaapinigaazoyang
mookimaazoyang endaso mooka'ang.

Ge-mooka'am giizis
babasikaweyang mashkiigong
mooshka'agwiinjiseg mii mashkawaandeg
anishinaabe babaapagidanaamod zaaga'iganing.

Gimookojigemin
giizhigag mookodamang
mazinikojiganag mookozhangwaa
mooka'asanjigoyang gijichaaginaanan.

Ganabaj gimookawaadamin
ezhi-anjidimaajimowaad
mii miinwaa gaa-mooka'amang
da-bagidenindamang.

Geyabi mookiingweniyang
mangodaasiyang
asabaatigoog aawiyang
asabikeyang awang.

After the Vote

Here in America
we are first people and settlers
free selves and taken slaves
voices rising anew with each dawn.

As the sun rises
we toss bones into the swamp
solid land emerges and
the first being breathes by the lake.

We have all been part of the carving
we cut away the days
sculpting the shape of spirits
to uncover the cache of our souls.

Maybe we cry
as the stories change
and what we uncover
needs a proper burial.

Still we appear
bravely centered
we are shuttles
making nets in the fog.

Animoomigo

Gaawiin gwa gidaawisiimin naasaab
aanawi bezhigowendamang mii
dash maamawi-babaama'adooyang
ge-giizhooninjiiyan niinizisaning
napaajiwendamang gakina gaawiin
makadewizisiiyaang gaye waabishkizisiiyang.

Gidaawimin zoogipog ziigwang
asigibii'iganan giizhigong
apane igo gii-pawaadamang
noondedibaajimoyang ji-ozhitooyang
gichi-mookomaan-akikeyang
maamakaadendaagwag miinawaa.

Riding Away

We are not the same being
but seamlessly we are thinking
as we ride to the same place
your warm hands in my hair
we are opposites
not black or white.

We are like snow in spring
numbers on days
forever in the dreaming
in need of stories
to make America
great again.

Gete-Mazinaagochigaans

Ginanaandawi-gikendaan gete-mazinaagochigaans
gii-apibii'igeyaan ji-mikawenindizoyaan
minisiwiyaan gaye gaawiin minisiwisiiyaan
onzaam mii ezhi-waawiinidizoyang
wiindamaazoyang giizhaajimoyang . . .
Robben Island azhenamawaawaad aaskigwan
Bedloe's Island azhenamawaawaad esan
mii waa-minisiinoowiyang azhegiiweyang
mayagitaagoziyang.

An Old Charm

You are examining an old charm
once written to remind myself
I am and I am not my own island
because as we rename ourselves
we tell the end of the story . . .
Robben Island is given back to the seals
Bedloe's Island is returned to the oysters
and we all become soldiers sent home
speaking each other's languages.

Māori Manaia

Gii-maamakaazaabandaan
nakeyaa giizhigong
nakeyaa anakwadong
maamakaamaadizid inaadizid.

Maagonaan banga'ang
onik debibidood aki
onik debibidood awan
maagobinidizod ininaamod.

Wii-maa'ikose anaamibiing
aadikwe'iged ozhigwanaad
aadikwe'iged ozhigiizhowed
gaagige-minawaanigoziwining.

Māori Manaia

She-He gazed in amazement
in the direction of the sky
in the direction of the clouds
spectacularly alive.

She-He feels a heartbeat
one arm touching the earth
one arm touching the mist
self-compressed and breathing.

She-He will go under the river
steering with a strong tail
steering commitments
into the afterlife.

Gaawiin maashi Giizhiitaasiiyaan

Gaawiin mashi giizhiitaasiiyaan
gaawiin zegizisiiyaan
gikenimagwaa Animikiig
didibaasewaad inde'ing
misko-ziibi baashkinedeg
gaa-ezhiwebag maada'oonidiyaang.
Wayaangawizijig aangodinong
wanishkweziwaagwen.
mii apane noondawiyan
giiweyendamawaanen.

This Is No Conclusion

This is no conclusion
I am not afraid
to know the Thunderbirds
swirling around my heart
a steaming red river
of history shared.
Sometimes the tame
are once again wild
and always you hear me
thinking of home.

Gimiigwechiwi'inininim / Acknowledgments

"Bangan Zoogipook" / "Silent Snowfall," "Ishkodensan" / "Matches," and "Zoongizaagi'diwin" / "Fierce Love" in A Poetry Congeries, Connotation Press: An Online Artifact, March 2019.

"Niizhosagoons gemaa Nisosagoons Daso-biboonagadoon" / "Two or Three Thousand Years" Broadsided Press, November 2018.

"Winiiam Aagimike" / "William Making Snowshoes," *Minnesota Conservation Volunteer* magazine, Minnesota Department of Natural Resources, November 2018.

"Winiiam Aagimike" / "William Making Snowshoes," Woodberry Poetry Archive and Peabody Museum of Archaeology & Ethnology, Harvard University, Fall 2018.

"Gaawiin o'o Dibendaagwasinoon" / "None of This Belongs Here," "Wanaanimizimagad" / "A Time of Confusion," and "Mamaangaashkaa Michigaming" / "The Surging Sea" in *The Recluse* 14, The Poetry Project, June 2018.

"Gimanaajitoomin Nibi: We Honor Water" appeared as part of an interactive online game *Honour Water* by Gloria Munoz for ivoh .org, August 29, 2016.

"People Were Created to be Loved" in *Sovereign Traces: Relational Constellation*, edited by Elizabeth LaPensée. Lansing: Michigan State University Press, 2018.

"Winiiam Aagimike" / "William Making Snowshoes," "Agoozimakakiig Idiwag" / "What the Peepers Say," "Jiikimaadizi" / "A Joyful Life," and "Mazinbii'amawaan" / "Sending Messages" in *New Poets of Native Nations*, edited by Heid Erdrich. Minneapolis: Graywolf Press, 2018.

"Bi Booniig" / "Let Them Be Here" in *Art Shanty Projects Literary Dev(ICE)*, edited by Cole Sarar, Minneapolis, 2018.

"Umpaowastewin" in *Ghost Fishing: An Anthology of Eco-Justice Poetry*, edited by Melissa Tuckey. Athens, University of Georgia Press, 2018.

"Aaniin Idamang?" in *(About that) Water is Life*, curated by Heid Erdrich, Main Gallery, Minnesota Center for Book Arts, June 9 through August 13, 2017.

"Umpaowastewin" in *Poetry*, Winter 2016.

"Bingwi-nanaandawi'iwe-nagamon" / "A Sandy Healing Song" in "Stories of Native Presence and Survivance in Commemoration of the 151st Anniversary of the Sand Creek Massacre," *Common-Place: The Journal of Early American Life* 16, no. 1 (Fall 2015).

"Umpaowastewin." Eat Local: Read Local. Milwaukee, Wisconsin, April 2015.

"Waanimazinbii'iganike" / "Writing Images in Circles" also appears in *Picturing Worlds: Visuality and Visual Sovereignty in Contemporary Anishinaabe Literature* by David Stirrup. Lansing: Michigan State University Press, 2020.

About the Author

Margaret Noodin received an MFA in Creative Writing and a PhD in English and Linguistics from the University of Minnesota. She is currently a professor of English and American Indian Studies at the University of Wisconsin–Milwaukee, where she also serves as the director of the Electa Quinney Institute for American Indian Education. She is the author of *Bawaajimo: A Dialect of Dreams in Anishinaabe Language and Literature* and *Weweni* (Wayne State University Press, 2015), a collection of bilingual poems in Ojibwe and English. Her poems and essays have been anthologized and published in *New Poets of Native Nations, Sing: Poetry from the Indigenous Americas, Poetry, The Michigan Quarterly Review, Water Stone Review* and *Yellow Medicine Review*. She is co-editor of *The Papers of the Algonquian Conference* and is an advocate for education and community engagement through relevant research and teaching.